The Green Room
Wisdom for Every Stage

Tony Hall, Sr.

JT Publishing House
www.jtpublishinghouse.com

Copyright © 2020 by Tony Hall, Sr.

Published by JT Publishing Spartanburg, South Carolina
www.jtpublishinghouse.com

No part of this publication may be reproduced, stored in a retrieval system, or transmitted in any form or by any means, electronic, mechanical photocopying, recording, scanning, or otherwise, except as permitted under Section 107 or 108 of the 1976 United States Copyright Act, without either the prior written permission of the author or authorization through payment of the appropriate per-copy fee to the Copyright Clearance Center, Inc. 222 Rosewood Drive, Danvers, MA 01923, 978-750-8400, fax 978-646-8600, or on the Web at www.copyright.com. Requests to the author for permission should be addressed to the Permissions Department, Tony Hall, Sr.

Limit of Liability / Disclaimer: The advice and strategies contained herein may not be suitable for your situation. You should consult with a professional where appropriate. Neither the Publisher nor the Author shall be liable for any loss of profit or any other commercial damages, including but not limited to special, incidental, consequential, or other damages.

Readers should be aware that Internet websites offered as citations and/or sources for further information may have changed or disappeared between the time this was written and when it is read. All rights reserved.

Scriptures taken from the Holy Bible, New International Version®, NIV®. Copyright © 1973, 1978, 1984, 2011 by Biblica, Inc.™ Used by permission of Zondervan. All rights reserved worldwide. www.zondervan.com The "NIV" and "New International Version" are trademarks registered in the United States Patent and Trademark Office by Biblica, Inc.™

Scripture taken from the New King James Version®. Copyright © 1982 by Thomas Nelson. Used by permission. All rights reserved.

JT Publishing House books and products are available through most bookstores.
To contact JT Publishing House, visit www.jtpublishinghouse.com.

Hall, Sr., Tony
The green room: wisdom for every stage/ Tony Hall, Sr.
South Carolina: JT Publishing House, 2020.

ISBN 978-0-9966300-2-3 (paperback) – ISBN 978-0-9966300-4-7 (ebook)
Library of Congress Cataloging-in-Publication Data: in progress

Printed in the United States of America

10 9 8 7 6 5 4 3 2 1

Dedication

To my queen, the absolute love of my life.

Foreword

There is not a person today who doesn't need a voice in their life.

I am not speaking of the voice of God—His voice is a given, and something we must all possess. Without the voice of God, we are on a spin cycle, lacking the knowledge we need to get out of motion.

However, in addition to the voice of God, there is a need for a mentor. A Godly person with divine wisdom, someone who loves you enough to speak into your life even if it hurts, someone who shows you where and how to get off the crazy, out of control, spin cycle. That person is Bishop Tony Hall, Sr.

Tony has been a personal friend of mine for many years. We affectionately refer to each other as "my brother from another mother." He has been a voice many times for our sons, giving them words of wisdom, advice, encouragement, and pure friendship.

Tony is living proof that one can survive the brutalities of life—the pains of abuse and disappointment. He determined, many years ago, to move beyond the scars of his past and allow God to turn his messed-up life into a ministry.

God's anointing and wisdom have equipped Tony Hall to become a much-needed voice in our world today.

You may be a struggling young person trying to figure out who you are, or perhaps you are in the middle of a failing marriage. Maybe you are an overwhelmed minister of the gospel, distracted by the issues of life, or you could be seeking wisdom for the next decade. Regardless of where you are in life, allow the concepts within this book to create a path to liberty, learning, and deliverance for you. Allow the wisdom Tony has acquired to help you prepare for your next stage of life.

Get ready; wisdom is going to help you turn your mess into a miracle!

Mike Cox
Senior Pastor
Crossroads Apostolic Church

Acknowledgments

First, I want to thank the Lord Jesus Christ; you have loved me unconditionally for the past 61 years of my life. Whether I was up or down, you still worked your will in my life. This book and everything I do give honor to you. Thank you for allowing me to continue making an impact and showing the world Jesus!

I want to thank everyone who came into my life at every juncture. To every pastor, teacher, and individual, thank you for making me a better person.

To my children, thank you for growing up with me and still becoming great individuals. I especially want to thank you and your spouses for all of my grandchildren and great-grandchildren! You all help me love individuals more than I could imagine.

I also want to thank all of you who count me as and call me your father. You all taught me how to become a better spiritual father, and you have helped me touch people all over the world.

Special love and thanks to Apostle Henry Alexander and Dr. Marty. Since we met in Nigeria, you two have been our greatest cheerleaders—during our time as pastors and now as retired pastors. Thank you for pushing me when necessary, you always spoke to the greatness we couldn't see in ourselves. Your example, as spiritual parents, helped us be better to the people God entrusted to us.

Special love and appreciation to Pastor Shari Fuller and Pastor David Johnson, for the past 30+ years, you have helped me dream. You let me speak wisdom in your lives, without judgment. Many spiritual sons and daughters have come and gone, but you two remain. I will always love and pray for you.

Lastly, I want to thank the world's greatest wife, my queen of 42 years! Denise, everything I am, and everything I have accomplished in my life, I'm thankful you were there.

There's an episode of Sanford and Son, where Fred disguises himself and speaks into an earpiece for Grady. Grady's date couldn't see Fred and continued to believe he was the owner of the words he shared.

Similarly, the world gets a chance to listen and look at me. However, I look and listen to you. Thank you

Acknowledgments

for remaining in my ear, telling me the greatness and ability you see in me. This book is dedicated to you because you gave life a shot with me.

Everyone said we'd never make it, and I'm sure there were times you wanted to walk away. Yet, you persisted. You have remained, and now we have a beautiful life.

The world is not ready for the new and improved Tony and Denise Hall, but we are getting ready to do more, see more, and achieve more than even we could have imagined.

I love you more every day, and I'm always shocked at how my love grows each night. I love you, and I thank you for sharing me with the world!

Table of Contents

Welcome to the Green Room
Preparing for Life's Stages
13

Wisdom Chronicles
What is Wisdom?
21

The GPS for Believers
Where are You Headed?
29

Behind the Scenes
Preparation for Marriage, Freedom is Not Free
33

Four-Part Stage
Shift Your Expectations and
Identify the Appropriate Box
39

Find Your Place at the Table
Bring Your Seat to the Stage
53

The Stages of the Green Room
Through the Years
63

Endorsements
107

About the Author
109

Welcome to the Green Room
Preparing for Life's Stages

"The preparations of the heart in man, and the answer of the tongue, is from the Lord. All the ways of a man are clean in his own eyes, but the Lord weigheth the spirit. Commit thy works unto the Lord, and thy thoughts shall be established."
Proverbs 16:1-3 (KJV)

When the curtain is pulled back, and the lights are pointed center stage, all that matters is the performance. Sitting on the edge of their seats with high anticipation, everyone's eyes are fixed on the stage. They are ready for the performance of a lifetime.

Simultaneously, the performer stands, appearing confident and sure that the rendition will be one for the ages.

During that moment, no one discusses with the

performer what it took to get to the stage. No one asks about fears they overcame, lessons they had to learn, or hardships they had to endure.

All that matters is the performance.

I've been a part of several world-changing ministries throughout my 40+ year career. While everyone gets excited about the performance, my excitement always occurred when I received backstage access to the green room.

I've never been crystal clear as to why it's called the green room because not one of the rooms, as far as I can remember, was ever painted green. However, the conversations I had during that window of time served as preparation for the stage.

The green room's importance to the performer is significant. In many cases, the room's contents are strategically placed to ensure hospitality and exude thoughtfulness.

More specifically, before the star arrives at the venue, his or her handlers are aware of all the necessary items needed to ensure the individual feels accommodated.

Some people like a specific type of water, nuts, or towels, and some have preferences about the

Welcome to the Green Room

temperature.

For example, I know a well-respected Christian performer who likes soft, classical music playing in the background when they arrive for an event. I know another Christian performer who refuses to practice or warm-up if the microphone they prefer has not been in place at least 24-hours before their arrival.

Then, there's the performer who requires the smell of imported oil and pictures of their family along the walls. There's a lot of preparation, and I can imagine the people managing the events don't sleep for weeks.

Interestingly, the individuals conducting the preparations very rarely, if ever, inquire about the requests of the performers as they enter into the green room.

However, they are aware that the quality of the performance depends upon the groundwork for the big event.

I hope to help prepare you for life's stages by sharing the experiences of each decade of my life, and as you dig into the pages of this book, my prayer is that you can't put down this book and that you find information to help you no matter your age.

I'd like to encourage you to lean into the messages throughout this book and allow the information to serve as your event planner.

There will likely be messages that challenge you and prompt you to burn this book or request a refund.

If it's rubbing you the wrong way, I encourage you to reread the messages again, explore your feelings, and question what the results could be in the next stage of life, should you choose not to deal with your findings.

I have found that sometimes, in the green room, you are going to hear how you were off-key, or that you blew the performance in the last show.

Don't let your arrogance and dysfunction cause you to reject wise counsel. Counsel could be the right lever to propel you into stardom.

As I complete *The Green Room: Wisdom for Every Stage*, I must admit I was unprepared for the feelings and emotions I have experienced as I scanned through the years of my life.

However, being able to lean into both my accomplishments and failures is a powerful place to sit, and knowing that God has remained with me through it all is both humbling and liberating.

Welcome to the Green Room

I have made a lot of mistakes along this journey, but God's grace has covered me, and it has allowed me time in my green room to prepare for the next stage of life.

Therefore, I am sharing the pain I have experienced, how I fell on my face after mistakes I made, and how I got back up, went back inside the green room, and asked God to help me pull it together.

Much like the physical green room those taking the stage enter, I believe we all need time in the green room.

We have various experiences in our lives that deserve preparation. I hope that through the words in this book, you will find information and nuggets that help you consider each phase of life from infancy to seventy-years-old—your own, personal, private green room that provides you wisdom for every stage of life.

Preparing for Life's Stage
When I was ten years old, Reverend Roy A. Allen from Chapel Hill Missionary Baptist Church served as my pastor. He was a dynamic preacher.

When he stood to preach, I stood and cried. His eloquence mesmerized me. After watching and listening to him, I knew what I wanted to do for the rest of my life.

By the time I was 12 years old, Reverend Allen had released a live album. He preached his sermon with passion and power.

At that time in my life, I was already exposed to drinking alcohol and smoking drugs. However, I knew the words to his album filler by filler, line by line. I could even say, "Amen," right on cue!

Before listening to his message, I always grabbed a pillowcase from my bed, and I tied it around my neck. I'd put on the only pair of black pants I owned, placed a mirror in front of me, and got my special "pastor seat" so that I could stand as he did in the pulpit.

The preparation was so much fun for me, but it was more fun than the performance itself. I enjoyed the details of the planning.

Now, retired at 61 years old, I realize I have been preparing my entire life, and I believe I have the wisdom and insight to effectively look back and realize how I arrived at the place I am today.

I have prepared for every major thing I have accomplished in my life. The phrase, "I left it up to

Welcome to the Green Room

God to get me here," is not applicable.

I worked alongside God.

God ordered my steps, He led me to and through some significant, earth-shaking moments, and then He allowed me to use those moments to touch thousands of people all over the world.

Today, I am a very happy husband to my queen, Denise. Denise and I have shared a lifetime of learning, growing, and evolving together. We have four great children, each with a wonderful spouse, fourteen grandchildren, and five great-grandchildren.

Personal perfection did not allow me to sustain my family; God sent me some incredible event planners to prepare my green room, people who have given me wisdom along the way.

Those individuals helped me get ready for the performance of fathering and maintaining a family. If God can do it for Denise and me, He can and will help you.

As babies, we don't know who we will become, but in a way, we are all world changers, touching thousands of lives during our lifetime. Therefore, preparation for our development is critical to ensure our readiness for the stage.

Maybe you are going to become a great father or mother, an anointed preacher, or a dynamite businessman or businesswoman; I assure you that success will not come by luck. Your preparation is vital.

I've witnessed amazing musicians with so much talent. However, some throw their lives away because they have not taken the necessary time to prepare. I want to be clear; I am not speaking to the performance they give to the crowd using their instrument.

I'm speaking specifically to the preparation to sustain or reach the level they desire—development of the heart and mind.

That type of preparation reminds me of the adage, "your gift will take you to the stage, but only your integrity will keep you once you've gotten there."

As you read, I believe you will see and learn things that will serve you well for your next stage of life.

I'd like to encourage you not to lose heart. Don't waste your ability to minister and share your gift because you are stuck in a stage of life. People are waiting for you.

Wisdom Chronicles
What is Wisdom?

"Wisdom is the principal thing; therefore, get wisdom, and with all thy getting get understanding."
Proverbs 4:7 (KJV)

For years, people have noted how wise I am.

Whenever someone brags about my wisdom, I smile.

However, internally I am laughing because I don't know how I've attained the wisdom I have; I just know God lives inside me.

I did not have a Godly mother or a fire-filled, preaching father. Truthfully, I grew up in dysfunction. I had God, and I allowed Him to take the wheel when Denise and I got married at 18 years old!

The Bible teaches in Proverbs 4:7, that "wisdom is

the principal thing; therefore, get wisdom, and with all thy getting get understanding" (KJV).

Using the scripture as the foundation, I firmly believe if you don't get the twins (wisdom and understanding) together, neither works for you. The two come as a duo, and they don't work well in isolation.

My definition of wisdom is the ability to navigate through tough times with truth.

When the scripture articulates that wisdom is the principle thing, it means it stands out above all things.

For example, people may ask you to pray for their health, but the root might be that the individual needs to take time to shift their lifestyle.

Therefore, wisdom is pointing our eyes towards the solution, even when we don't know which question to ask.

By age 9, I was bitten by the entrepreneur bug.

I sold newspapers for years, and then I started a barbeque business in my thirties. Some might argue that I had a gift to make money with my "side hustles."

After dropping out of school in the 9th grade, I soon realized that getting a 9-5 job wasn't going to work for me.

I made thousands of dollars with my homemade barbeque sauce; however, because I lacked wisdom, I was always broke.

My gifts always helped me to make money, but the absence of wisdom left me in lack.

When I look back at how it hurt my family, I still feel bad about it, which is why I say one must have wisdom and understanding.

As you grow in wisdom, you should pray that God sends you someone to help you in the areas of weakness. Again, wisdom points our eyes towards the solution when we don't know how or which question to ask.

When I finally grew into maturity, I learned that God gave me a wife to help me in my areas of weakness.

Back then, I saw her comments as a put down when she suggested plans to save our money. Today, I find her words as jewels and see them as a great blessing.

As a result, we are living our best life.

The Lack of Wisdom
In the book of Numbers, chapter 13, the Israelites are complaining and constantly beating up Moses for being dishonest and leading them to their deaths.

God speaks to Moses and tells him, pick out one leader from each tribe. I want you to send them into the land I promised, and I want to allow them to see what's coming if they can believe.

Moses told the spies, "Go into the land undercover, take your time, and see if the land is not going to be amazing for us when we go in."

The twelve spies went home and kissed their wives and children goodbye.

I can assume that many of the men believed the assignment would lead to death because they did not believe in Moses' ability to lead them. Some probably thought, why does it have to be me who goes into the place in which we are unfamiliar?

However, the men journeyed to the new land. After being in the area for 40 days, they returned to the camp.

Would they return with a good report of victory or an evil report of disgust and fear?

Wisdom Chronicles

Personally, I would have loved to have been a fly on the bags they carried back, to see what they really felt about the new land.

Nevertheless, the twelve spies, after traveling to the same land, seeing the same things, and engaging in the same experiences, returned with different opinions.

Ten of the men came back with an evil report.

They saw the land as being too much for them, so they gave it an F+ in all areas.

The other two spies used wisdom. When they returned, they were excited and wanted to go back and take over the land the same day.

What was the difference?

The difference was, the ten saw the land through their experiences and mentalities—a lack of wisdom.

The other two spies, using wisdom, understood what going into the promised land could mean for them. Because of their perception of the situation, they subdued the land.

Very similar, like many people I know, we grew up in the same county, under the same rules, some of us the same race, educated in the same classrooms, yet some become defeated by life while others live it up big!

It's all based on mentality.

I've learned, God cannot break our mentality. If we have a defeatist mentality or attitude, we will never break through the barriers of life.

Mentality has caused millions to die without seeing the land God set aside for them—their promised land.

I've met people from good families, with lots of money, and endless opportunities. However, for years I felt terrible because I had neither of those options, but the one thing that set us apart was wisdom.

Caleb and Joshua, two of the twelve spies, had wisdom. They knew God would take them into the land and give them the power and the strength to navigate through tough situations.

After all, He delivered them from Egypt.

The other ten men said the people were giants and saw them as grasshoppers.

Had the men returned to me with that information, I likely would have asked, "Who told you to interview people and ask what they thought about you?"

The ten wimps saw themselves as grasshoppers, and they spoke up for people who didn't know they were there.

It's all about mentality!

I often ask people, "Who told you that you were defeated?"

"Who told you that your marriage was over?"

"Who told you that you'd always be broke?"

"Who told you that you'd die young?"

"Who told you that you'd never have a child?"

As an ordained counselor in ministry, when people come into my office for counseling, I tell them to leave what they feel at the door and tell me what's happening specifically.

I know those words sound harsh, but feelings never help a bad situation.

During a counseling session, we are not there to talk

about feelings. We are there to talk about occurrences and how to straighten out the mess the individuals have gotten into.

I have learned that "10 things to help you not have problems," does not exist. However, if we pray for wisdom, we can rest knowing God will take the wheel of our lives and make us and things concerning us better.

When life says, "no," it is often our lack of wisdom that causes us to believe we are conquered, and where we are is where we will remain.

However, wisdom pushes us to prepare for victory because of what the Lord will do in our lives and the situation, giving us the ability to navigate through tough times with truth.

The GPS for Believers
Where are You Headed?

Wisdom shouts in the streets. She cries out in the public square. She calls to the crowds along the main street, to those gathered in front of the city gate: "How long, you simpletons, will you insist on being simpleminded? How long will you mockers relish your mocking? How long will you fools hate knowledge? Come and listen to my counsel. I'll share my heart with you and make you wise.
Proverbs 1:20-23 (NLT)

I spent nearly $600 on my touch screen radio, but my fascination was the GPS.

My intrigue with the GPS generated because my wife and I are retired, and we wanted to travel the country.

As such, I don't want to deal with the traps of the road. Some cites have secret tolls, causing visiting drivers to pay all kinds of money as they try to navigate around the city.

There are also accidents and traffic that impede our ability to travel, causing us to feel stuck with nowhere to go.

Cities also have police traps, which lead to speeding tickets and high levels of frustration. However, my GPS has a button that provides insight on routes to take in any city within the United States—that fact makes me excited to travel with my bride!

I program the setting to "no tolls," "mention accident warnings," and "warn me of police officers," and we are effectively off to our destination.

When I think about all the features of my GPS, I think about life, and how we can program our lives to live more productively. I think about the choices we make and how we choose to govern every day.

To me, wisdom is the GPS of life.

It allows us to get to our destination when we are lost.

Wisdom is the instructional booklet on how to put together the 1000-piece puzzle of life.

The GPS for Believers

Wisdom comforts us when feelings of loneliness or defeat try to creep in and cause us to wish we were never born.

Wisdom must be the GPS, the navigation system, for the life of a believer.

The Bible teaches us that wisdom cries in the streets. Wisdom cries aloud to the people who are going about their lives, trying to correct their ways.

I've been praying for wisdom since I was a young man, and I believe those prayers have allowed me to have a pretty great life.

Having wisdom as your compass doesn't mean you won't face roadblocks and challenges.

With 40 years of active ministry involvement, I have experienced and seen a lot of things. I have dealt with the stresses of ministry (some of which have kept me up at night).

The only thing I could rely on was wisdom. Wisdom kept and keeps me happy and whole.

Personally, I cannot imagine always having trial after trial in my marriage, or drama in my immediate family, that would drive me nuts. Yet, some people have settled into that type of drama, and it has become their norm. Help them, God!

To me, that type of acceptance indicates that those individuals do not have wisdom, and dysfunction continues to breed. Wisdom allows us to lean in and understand how to handle situations that arise.

I would encourage you to spend time in God's word, reading and learning about wisdom. There is wisdom for every stage of life, and without it, we continue to live fractured lives.

Choose wisdom and watch things shift in your life!

Behind the Scenes
Preparation for Marriage, Freedom is Not Free

"Marriage should be honored by all, and the marriage bed kept pure, for God will judge the adulterer and all the sexually immoral." Hebrews 13:4 (NIV)

Denise and I wed Saturday, October 15, 1977.

Early that morning, I made a trip to the barbershop.

As I waited for my barber, my mind raced thinking about how married life would be with Denise. I no longer had to sneak around with my girlfriend when her father wasn't home.

I took a loud gasp and said, "In a few hours, I'll finally be free!"

I felt like I would be free from the church people who hated that Denise and I were getting married.

I thought I would be free from the criticism of my father about who I chose to marry, and free from people saying I was not good enough."

At my core, I believed I was going to be happy and free, and I thought life would be easy and comfortable moving forward.

I had no idea that being free came with such a high cost!

However, I really didn't have a clue; I was only 18 years old.

Proverbs 22:15 reads, "foolishness is bound up in the heart of a child; The rod of discipline [correction administered with Godly wisdom and lovingkindness] will remove it far from him" (AMP).

At the time, I didn't realize it, but I had foolishness in my heart, but discipline would soon remove it!

Once Denise and I got married, I quickly realized my problem was immaturity.

I didn't have a good example of being a Godly husband, but I loved God and my young, beautiful wife.

It took a lot of wisdom and prayer to correct the

Behind the Scenes

foolishness in my heart.

We received evictions, car repossessions, and days of hunger in our early years of marriage.

One of the things that helped us was moving away from Detroit, where we both grew up.

Moving 1,600 miles away from everyone and everything drove the foolishness out of our hearts.

We couldn't run to mom or dad.

We couldn't leave when we were ticked off with each other.

We could only cry out to God. Crying out to God, was the very thing we needed. Sometimes parents won't allow the rod of correction to drive foolishness out of their children's lives, and it causes greater significance for the child in the long run.

By the time we were 23 years old, we faced a time where our test had become the rod of correction.

To this day, I believe the correction we received during that time of our lives produced wisdom in us.

At the time, my wife was pregnant with April.

Well, I'd met some slick preachers who were in town. They talked me into coming to work for them.

Gullibly, I left my good, managerial job at McDonald's, to work for them. I lost my insurance, my vacation time, and the owner was so disappointed, as I was the first black manager in San Antonio.

The preachers never paid me one dime of the money they promised.

Shortly after that, my wife went into labor. Again, we no longer had insurance, but we had "faith," right!

I told my wife it was against the law for the hospital to refuse her care because she was in labor. That was the foolishness talking.

I dropped her off at the hospital and went back to work.

The hospital called me and said, "Young man, in order for us to take care of your wife, we need $700."

That kind of money, at that time, was like $7,000,000; I knew I didn't have that kind of money, so I had to take my wife to the county hospital, which was not ideal.

After 48 hours of waiting, I took her back to the

Behind the Scenes

same hospital. By that time, April was drowning in her mother's womb. When we returned, I raised so much confusion they finally took her back to check her.

A young intern came from the back and asked me to follow him in the family room. There, he told me someone was going to die, my wife, my baby, or both!

He asked me to sign the paperwork to abort the pregnancy, so they could place all their efforts on saving my wife.

I remember standing there alone, unsure about what to do. We went to a large church at the time, but no one came to the hospital to help us.

We were alone—it was God and us.

I asked to see my wife.

She was in so much pain that they gave her medication to calm her down. I held her hand, and I turned my face to the wall. I made God a vow that day if He'd give us our child, we'd make sure we led her in the ways of the Lord.

I refused to sign the paper, April was born, my wife survived, and we kept our vow to God.

Whatever immaturity problem I had, the pressure and thought of losing my wife drove it out from me. I gained my freedom, but it came with falling flat on my face.

I had to allow God to mold me into His desired image. I am grateful for the work He has done in my life, and the wisdom He gave me at this stage of life.

Four-Part Stage
Shift Your Expectations and
Identify the Appropriate Box

"Their purpose is to teach people wisdom and discipline, to help them understand the insights of the wise. Their purpose is to teach people to live disciplined and successful lives, to help them do what is right, just, and fair." Proverbs 1:2-3 (NLT)

Every stage has sections, and each section is designed for certain people. Everyone doesn't have the same level of access.

I would argue that the same should be true in our lives.

I have encountered so many different types of people throughout my life, and I have learned that everyone does not need the same level of commitment. If we try to give the same time, energy, and space to everyone we meet, we will likely live very unhappy and displeasing lives.

Therefore, I have four mental boxes that I place people into: the intimate box, the professional box, the toleration box, and the never again in life box. For me, the boxes help me have a healthy balance of what I give and expect from others.

Everyone, and I mean everyone, who comes into Anthony Q. Hall's life, will be placed into one of the four boxes.

Individuals in my life will never know which box I've placed them into, however, knowing allows me to handle them accordingly.

Box #1: The Intimate Box
The intimate box includes my go-to people.

When we are together, we both win 100% of the time.

We are not trying to take advantage of each other; instead, we show each other mutual love and respect.

The blessing is, this box has the least amount of people in it.

If there were a lot of people in this box, dysfunction

Four-Part Stage

would likely emerge, and things might fall apart when the first challenge arises.

In this box, keeping people out who are not totally committed to you is vital.

Pastor David Johnson is my closest friend, spiritual son, and brother in the whole world. Our relationship changes, but in the end, I'm still a father to him.

Roughly twenty years ago, we had a major blow out. I was, of course, hurt and refused to speak to David, ever again, like a teenager.

Then one day, he called and left me a message saying, "I am not going to let you destroy what we have. We are going to disagree, but that should never end our amazing relationship."

After hearing his message and engaging in a conversation, we have been super close since. Truthfully, some of my children are not in my intimate box. However, David Johnson remains.

Box #2: The Professional Box
The professional box is the most comfortable box for people in my life.

Being a pastor, spiritual father, life coach, businessman, and now a retiree, I come in contact with a lot of people.

Therefore, I treat most of the people in my life, my past, and my future, professionally.

We are going to have some great times together, and they will feel my love and concern for them, but know this, it's a professional relationship. If I try to make them an intimate friend, I will make a horrible mistake.

How many friends have you had where things seemed so well until correction, or going against something they stand for or believe in was on the table?

The reason it went south is that the individual is placed in the wrong box.

In my professional box, I stand my ground, and I allow the other individual to stand their ground, and should the relationship go south, it's alright because we are in a professional space.

I know some of you may be thinking, "Come on, Bishop Hall, are you saying that I should be fake in my relationships?"

"Absolutely not!"

Four-Part Stage

However, I am suggesting that you remain vigilant about not allowing people to move into your intimate box without proving over time they belong there.

I've had people who were close to me in ministry disregard me due to a position I took on an issue.

The shift in our relationship could have been devastating. However, because my expectations were appropriately placed, it lessened the implications.

I can tell you from experience that there's nothing like a good challenge to let you see what kind of friend you really have.

When situations happen that bring drama, cut your losses, and move the individual to the appropriate box in your life.

Box#3: Toleration Box
The toleration box helps me stay sane!

I used to be a person who allowed everyone to have personal time in my life and bring all their drama into my space.

I believe that it takes courage to live a great life, and most people just don't have the courage to be able to live the life they desire.

Because of that, they hurt, hate, and become jealous of people who have a functional life.

Moreover, they often look for someone to blame for their unhappiness.

I will always love and show compassion for people in my life, but the individuals in my toleration box are sometimes hard to deal with.

As a pastor, I hate to say it, but there are some people I am really tolerating rather than loving. I will hug and pray with them, but in my world of boxes, I'm tolerating them.

If I don't place them in the toleration box, the worst in me will likely surface.

To effectively enact this box in my life, I had to love myself enough to stop allowing others to establish my life's plan.

The truth is, the people we tolerate don't have the courage to change their lives, and there's nothing we can do to demand they shift their behavior.

When I was younger, that notion really bothered me.

However, as I grew older, I settled into the truth that James shared in chapter 1, verse 4.

Four-Part Stage

He writes, "Each one is tempted when he is dragged away, enticed and baited [to commit sin] by his own [worldly] desire (lust, passion) (AMP)."

Meaning, people have their own free will, but their desires tempt them.

To be honest, I always thought that if I had an opportunity to sit and give people my time, we could pray, believe, and confess change, and things would disappear out of the air.

The truth is, we can pray, confess, and believe, but the individuals we deal with must break the chains of dysfunction in their lives to have the new, amazing life they desire.

I'm convinced that a lot of people will not do what it takes to live such a life.

Therefore, I place them in the toleration box, so I can continue the life I'm trying to live—one of peace and prosperity.

Box#4: Never Again in Life
The fourth box is the box I need prayer for, but it is also the most important to me.

The fourth box includes the people I never have to

see again in life! While many may choose not to acknowledge it, I believe we all have encountered people that we would be fine never seeing again.

I have unfortunately experienced some very unpleasant people, some of which who have brought unpleasant circumstances to my front door. For that, I could go without seeing those individuals ever again!

However, the never again in life box is important because it includes people who genuinely need prayer. Likewise, I have to pray and ask God to keep my heart pure so that I can offer sincere prayers on their behalf.

I have found that by keeping my heart right it positions me to be more concerned about the circumstance and less entangled in my personal feelings.

I believe having the never again in life box is critical. By not having this type of box, we open ourselves up to long-term damage that we are likely unable to recover from indefinitely.

In 2008 we moved to North Carolina to help a pastor with a ministry. We loved the people, and we felt loved. After five years of drama and other unfortunate situations, I felt like it was time for us to leave.

Four-Part Stage

I went to the leader and told him and his wife that we had decided to leave.

I told him that when we moved to North Carolina, we were friends and partners in ministry.

When he asked me what happened, I told him that if he would give me 45 days to remove everything out of my office, pay me all monies owed, and not trash my name (as I heard him do others), then we could sit down as friends to discuss my concerns.

Our agreement lasted about one week after we left the ministry.

Not only did it go bad quickly, but other things happened as well.

Knowing all that transpired during that situation, I felt myself become angry and bitter in my heart.

When you're in that type of situation, it changes who you are, and you want revenge.

During that time, I was broke, lied to, and lied on. I was ready to retaliate against the person who not only offended me but also continued to say untrue things.

Then, he started to demean me on social media

subliminally. When I read things that were posted, I immediately replied with my truth!

When I replied to anything, my baby daughter would call and tell me to remove my comments.

Eventually, I decided to take matters to an attorney because the organization was refusing compensation.

After providing my attorney with the appropriate paperwork, they believed we had a straightforward case, and they were ready to proceed.

I remember that afternoon, my cousin called to check-in with me. I shared my excitement for justice.

Rather than celebrating with me, my cousin, who is not a preacher, said, "Cuz, do not go back to the attorney's office to sign the paperwork.

I believe that if you let the situation go, let him have that money he owes you, God will give you seven times what you lost."

At the moment, I was furious!

I was upset with my daughter for encouraging me to remove my comments, with my cousin for giving me a word from the Lord, the pastor because he wronged me, and I was upset with God because he

Four-Part Stage

didn't strike the preacher down! I felt like my wife and I were alone, without anyone on our side.

However, my daughter knew that I had the respect of people all over the world, and if I let my pain show on Facebook, then the person who it would hurt was me. She was protecting my name and legacy.

My cousin had unfortunately had a similar experience, so he personally knew the pain I was facing.

To that end, he also knew the consequences of dealing with people who have wronged you. He wanted me to know that it's easy to preach, but it's harder to live and practice it every day.

God wanted me to trust Him. After all, He sees and knows the beginning and the end.

I had to trust that He would bring healing from the hurtful situation. God was more concerned about my effectiveness than my level of comfort.

Because He is sovercign, He looks at our painful times and gets excited knowing it's all going to work together for our good because we love him and are called according to His purpose.

This situation occurred six years ago, and I have

thankfully moved away from the original place of hurt and pain, and God has brought all that I thought I lost back more than twenty times.

I have placed that pastor in my never again in life box, but I still pray for his soul.

Ultimately, the never again in life box is for people who brought great harm to you, co-workers, ex-lovers, family members, or friends.

Although we could live life without seeing those particular individuals again, it is still pertinent that we model after Jesus.

Jesus never said to pray for your friends.

He knew it would be easy to pray for those who love you; therefore, Jesus constantly told His disciples to pray for their enemies.

The whole concept of praying for your enemies helps you more than it helps them—it's impossible to hate someone you pray for.

By praying for those who bring the most conflict to our lives, we are inviting and welcoming a pleasant and calm lifestyle into our space.

I encourage you to employ wisdom and generate

Four-Part Stage

boxes for the people who take residence in your life. Having boxes will bring you peace of mind and allow you to have the appropriate expectations of others.

Tony Hall, Sr.

Find Your Place at the Table
Bring Your Seat to the Stage

"All the people assembled with a unified purpose at the square just inside the Water Gate. They asked Ezra the scribe to bring out the Book of the Law of Moses, which the Lord had given for Israel to obey." Nehemiah 8:1 (NLT)

Years ago, if you desired answers to everyday problems, you'd go to the town square to see men of wisdom and power.

Those individuals were making laws, handling disputes, teaching, and training the older and younger men about the laws and statutes of the day.

Today, we unfortunately have a generation that has no understanding of how life works. I am convinced that the lack of understanding occurs because those of us with lived experience have not created a table where life's challenges or the "how-to" guide is shared.

If we are honest with ourselves, there are things we missed or didn't accomplish because we can't know what we don't know.

I would argue that every decade of life needs a table to come to for wisdom.

From birth to age twenty, boys and girls need an opportunity to listen to the conversation. While most topics are above their pay grade, if you will, the power of being at the table will provide them a standard of what to expect from life.

At the table, not only will they hear what to do, but they will also learn what not to do.

Wise parents will ensure that the people in front of their children confirm what they are teaching their children. After all, it is the parent's responsibility to teach their children the tenants of wisdom.

If parents aspire to raise wise children, they must act as their wisdom and have men and women of power and those who have failed (because failure is an important concept to learn) at their table.

Twenty-one to thirty-year-old individuals need a table designed to answer questions.

Because the 20-year-old is often focused on learning,

Find Your Place at the Table

the questions they ask are essentially helping them form their opinion.

Their opinion allows them to generate ideas on how they want to enact their beliefs into their lives.

As I shared, in my twenties, I worked for the church.

Working for the church allowed me direct access to my pastors.

From them, I was able to see how they interacted with people, and I was able to ask them questions that ultimately helped me become a better husband, father, and minister.

When our 20-year-old men and women ask questions from people in their age group, they will form habits that will perpetuate a mindset of selfishness.

Conversely, when a 20-year-old find their way to the table where wisdom is served, they will build relationships with people who will make a commitment to help them grow and reach their desired level of success.

During the thirty-one to forty age bracket, men and women should serve at the table, as the only way to destroy selfishness is through service.

Tony Hall, Sr.

Service allows the individual performing the act to become a better person.

Still, it also provides the individual being served the opportunity to share nuggets of wisdom that will likely help the server change the world.

My wife and I became great servants in our thirties. People would call us flunkies and brown nose kids, but our service to others helped us learn how to serve each other better in our marriage.

For us, service produced a great marriage, but it also impacted our parenting.

Today, I see servanthood in our children and grandchildren, as they work with people within their church and professional communities.

Our willingness to serve at the table prompted men and women all over the world to open doors that allowed us to travel and have a greater impact on others.

All of our successes came from our willingness to serve in our thirties. If you are currently in your thirties, I would strongly recommend that you find a place at someone's table, whether it's at work, church, or in your community, and serve.

Find Your Place at the Table

Don't look for compensation.

The rewards will come, and those rewards will set you up to become higher than anyone in your circle. The individuals who called us flunkies then refer to us as a great man and woman of God now!

Forty-one to fifty-year-old individuals come to the table with answers. After being at the table to ask questions, learn, and faithfully serve, discipline has likely been developed, and you are equipped to find answers to questions.

This stage of life is often met with humility, and people at the table notice the confidence and willingness you have to serve and help others find the answers.

In my forties, God placed us in a predominately white church organization.

Due to my upbringing, the pain I experienced as a child, and as an African American man, I thought I was the least likely individual to be involved in that situation.

During that time, I saw and experienced things that would have made most black men my age, picket, or be ready for a fight.

However, as a servant, I was able to help a lot of men and women to come to terms with various issues they were experiencing around race and diversity, and we are friends to this day.

What I learned is that I was coming to the table with answers.

Yes, it was uncomfortable at times, but it was a necessary part of the journey. Those uncomfortable moments placed a mandate on my growth and development as a man and as a leader.

Once, while a part of that particular organization, I recall being invited to preach in a certain city. When I walked on the stage, everyone in the first five rows started to gather their purses and belongings and walk to the back of the church.

I later learned I was the first black man to preach at a service.

I could have reacted, but I knew that because God placed me at an uncomfortable table, I was there to serve the people, help support their questions with wisdom and understanding, and let God be glorified.

After the service, the pastor told me that he'd pay me, and I didn't have to come back.

Find Your Place at the Table

"Absolutely not, I'll be back tomorrow night," I said.

The next night, the back of the church was filled when I got up to preach, so I picked up the podium and walked to the back of the church.

It was tough to stand and deliver the word at first, but God's glory filled the room, and we experienced a true move of God.

At the 40-year mark, you should have enough life experience, that you don't give up quickly, and when you get to any table, you will have what it takes to influence others.

From fifty-one to sixty years of age, we should be able to sit at the table and locate the gifts and talents of individuals and affirm their contributions.

By the time I turned 50 years old, I felt like I'd figured out life and love.

I also felt like I could handle some of life's most challenging issues.

We faced success, failure, abundance, lack, good health, and heart attacks by fifty, and as a result, we were mature.

Therefore, I believed I could see the gifts and talents

in others and honor their value.

Individuals sixty-one to seventy are needed at the table because of their deep sense of being and contribution.

There is a calm presence this group brings to situations that provides guidance and direction for generations prior.

When we reached retirement, we were thrilled.

Retirement is so exciting to us because we have raised kids, built businesses, started churches, evangelized all over the world, met new people in airports and malls, and now, our years of labor are over.

Everything we attempted for the past 43 years we now have an opportunity to enjoy.

We have reached a point in which we don't feel that we have anything to prove.

We are satisfied with what we have accomplished, and we have turned our hearts totally to making the Kingdom of God look good.

For so many years, we have tried to prove our work and place in the kingdom. A lot of it was peer pressure and trying to work our way up to certain positions that organizations offered.

However, after being promoted, it never gave us the sense of satisfaction we believed it would.

Now that we are retired, we agree with the psalmist David, who noted how beneficial it is to look at the highs and lows of life.

David measured his successes and failures, and although God took away his ability to build the temple and gave it to his son, David did not become bitter.

For some, that type of loss would have destroyed their ego.

Not David!

Sitting at the table with calmness penetrating throughout his being, he said, "I have set my affections on the house of my God, and I will give of my own things to make the house of God look amazing."

When we reach our 60-year-old mark, we should not feel isolated, believing, or thinking that we do not matter or that our time has passed.

Rather, we should be in a position to offer value to

those at the table.

Finding your place at the table, at all ages and stages of life, is wise. It shows that you are concerned with your evolvement and that you want to build and leave something in this world of substance and value.

I encourage you to find your seat at the table, and should you find yourself lacking a table or a seat, I recommend building your own!

The Stages of the Green Room
Through the Years

"Teach us to number our days so that we may gain a heart of wisdom." Psalm 90:12 (NIV)

Gaining a heart of wisdom is critical to our growth and development as human beings, and it is required for all ages and stages of life. From infancy to death, wisdom serves as a critical component of how we evolve and who we become.

From infancy to twenty, we are reliant upon our parents for every need and desire; from twenty-one to thirty, we are beginning to learn more about ourselves and our view of the world.

From thirty-one to forty, we are laying the groundwork for the life we desire to experience long-term.

From forty-one to fifty, we are beginning to share what we have learned with others to help influence their journey.

From fifty-one to sixty, we have established who we are, and our mindset begins to shift to the type of legacy we want to leave.

From sixty-one to seventy, our wealth, health, and solidifying the legacy becomes paramount.

At each decade of my life, I have been allowed to look back and see how important preparation is for each stage of life.

The lessons we experience and learn in one stage become the groundwork for continuing along the path. Our lessons of each stage of life indicate things we need to plow and tear down. If we allow wisdom to guide us, we live a fulfilled life that ultimately leads to honor.

The Brain-dead Years: Ages 0-20
From the time a child is born until he or she reaches 20 years old, I consider those years the brain-dead years because the brain is not fully developed. Therefore, it's the responsibility of parents to act as their child/ren's wisdom.

It's interesting because, as human beings, we are fully capable of obtaining knowledge.

The Stages of the Green Room

However, I'm convinced a lot of the dysfunction we witness stems from us being driven by gaining knowledge, while we have very limited wisdom.

The implications our lack of wisdom has on children is huge.

During this time, children are extremely impressionable. They also have a clean slate, so as fathers and mothers, we are crafting and drafting the foundational stories of their lives.

Not employing wisdom for our children during this stage of their life, is like leaving their green room empty, causing them to figure out which elements belong.

An empty green groom establishes the premise for a fractured life.

Therefore, surrounding children with wisdom helps them break through the noise to live a whole and healthy lifestyle.

As a child, I experienced so much trauma and pain. Looking back, it is not surprising to me that I wanted to take my life by the time I was a teenager.

My mother died when I was seven years old, and my father suffered from bitterness. For years, he stayed mad at our pastor for forgetting to announce that my mother needed blood to survive.

The posture of his heart brought dysfunction into our home.

My father moved his family from Georgia into our home. They were there to help take care of my siblings and me.

While I know his decision was rooted in love and needing support. It was not the best decision for our family. My dad's family was filled with alcoholics, which made matters worse.

In the movie Armageddon, a man inquires about the condition of the earth, and they respond, "worst case scenario!"

That was the Hall home, "worst case scenario!"

My father stopped attending church.

By the time I turned 11 years old, I had smoked my first joint, which caused me to start chasing my next high—despite the sickness that came afterward. Soon thereafter, and soon started trying to mask my pain with sex and drugs.

I don't hold my father's actions against him.

The Stages of the Green Room

As a matter of fact, in my first book, I encourage men and women to find out their father's story because "fathers hurt too!"

While I was exposed to a lot as a child, my father still made certain that my siblings and I learned the importance of hard work and taking care of the home.

My brothers and I knew how to cook, clean, iron, and take care of the house. My father also taught us how to pay bills.

Every Monday night, he forced us to sit with him around the kitchen table, and he pulled out his old black shoebox.

He'd take the bills and explain what he was paying.

Although we didn't fully understand what he was doing and were totally bored, Clarence Hall wanted his sons to understand their role, should we have a wife die young, and need to cover certain responsibilities.

He also made sure we had jobs.

I had a paper route as a youngster. I went door-to-door delivering newspapers on the streets of Detroit.

Tony Hall, Sr.

Although a rough time in my life, I gained an unmatched work ethic, and I learned how to survive.

My father also made sure my siblings and I went to church (despite him no longer going) and had other positive role models in our lives. I affectionally referred to them as the Dream Team, and I thanked God for them daily!

Having their guidance helped me handle some of the anger I had bottled up inside.

I tell parents all the time, if your child/ren experience trauma in their lives, they need professional help as soon as possible.

When my mom passed, and my dad became a 33-year-old, single parent, my Uncle Estes was the man who truly came to my father's rescue.

My uncle purchased a house down the street from us and served as my father's eyes and ears when he was at work.

He took us to baseball games, football games, amusement parks, and even to work at times.

He knew that he couldn't be our father, and he certainly couldn't be our mother, but he held up my father's hands when he needed it.

The Stages of the Green Room

Raising children is hard work. It's tough when doing it alone and even with a loving partner.

Denise and I did our best to rear our children according to Proverbs 22:6, "Train up a child in the way he should go [teaching him to seek God's wisdom and will for his abilities and talents], even when he is old he will not depart from it" (AMP).

Using this scripture as our foundation meant going to teach our children the ways of the Lord. It did not mean we perfectly raised our children, but we did our best to live by the following tenants, in an effort to put wisdom in their heads and hearts.

I believe these principles are solid pieces of information for both single-parent and two-parent households, as we all want our children to lead productive lives.

As parents, we tried our best to maintain a positive relationship in front of our children.

Married couples sometimes have disputes, and single parents may not always see eye to eye.

However, it's important to remember we are our children's wisdom, and maintaining a healthy relationship in front of them, being mindful of our words, and actions is key.

Tony Hall, Sr.

We did not serve as our children's buddies or friends.

While we want our children to talk to us and share their thoughts and concerns, as children and even as adults, we are clear that we are not their friends. Being our children's friends can make it difficult when correction needs to occur.

We also work like it depends on us, but we pray like it depends on God.

Because God knows all things, it's critical that we depend on the Holy Spirit to lead and guide as we raise our children.

My wife and I never led out of guilt. If our children ever see us leading from a guilty place, they will find it difficult to respect our words and choices.

While Denise and I served as the primary role models for our children, we were aware that it takes a village.

If for some reason you can't live the example you want for your children, find it in someone else and ask them to influence your seed.

Finally, stop beating yourself up for past mistakes. Do the best you can until you know better, then, as Mya Angelou says, "do better!"

The Stages of the Green Room

From infancy to twenty, as parents, it's critical that you establish the standard of your house, sow love and discipline, and lay the groundwork for success because they are soaking up everything that's happening around them.

Of course, they are going to make dumb decisions; we all did!

However, as a good parent, you have to remain on duty to quickly correct them so they can successfully move on to the next level.

Your children are in your hands, and it's your responsibility to give them the ability to survive in this crazy world. It's your job to serve as their wisdom.

A Time for Encouragement: Ages 21-30

Once an individual reaches 21-years of age, encouragement is often needed because the pressure of decision-making and leading life independently is beginning to settle in.

I like to encourage this group to use their time in the green room wisely, as this timeframe passes quickly.

Sometimes during this stage of life, people will overlook your mistakes, believing you will eventually turn the tide.

During this stage of life, the greatest gift you can give your parents is to lean into opportunities that allow you to gain wisdom.

This timeframe has a sneaky way of making you believe things last forever.

It's not true!

Beauty only lasts for a short time, and the older you become, the more your attractions to who people are will increase.

Likewise, during this time of your life, your sex drive is often high. I strongly encourage you to love yourself enough not to give pieces of yourself to undeserving individuals.

Lacking wisdom and integrity during this time can lead to emptiness.

Education is another important factor during this stage of life.

In my twenties, I didn't realize the value of education added to my life. As a high school dropout, I didn't realize or understand the doors that would be open to me had I given serious attention to my studies.

The Stages of the Green Room

My wife dropped out of school, but she made it a point to return to complete her high school diploma, and today she has a master's degree.

I also found it extremely difficult to hold my children to an expectation that I didn't honor myself.

I spent my twenties in survival mode because of the poor choices I made as a teenager.

I needed encouragement during this time in my life. I believe the right encouragement could have shifted my viewpoint and pushed me to try harder.

To that end, during this timeframe, pray every day for wisdom and watch God encourage your heart and increase the work of your hands.

It's All About Me, The Selfish Years: Ages 31-40
Studies show that the average age of couples going through their first divorce is 30 years old.

I often wonder why there are so many breakups during those years, as it seems like a great time to be alive.

Usually, during this time, educational achievements are met, and the newness of doing things your "own" way has settled.

However, I have found that many are devasted during this phase of life for a variety of reasons, and the at the root of a lot of the turmoil they are experiencing is selfishness.

When people in this age group come into my office, I generally hear excuse after excuse as to why the idea, the marriage, or the job failed. Yet, as we peel back the layers, time after time we discover that the root cause is selfishness.

Now, I am not suggesting that every case is selfishness, but in my experience, it's often a culprit.

I heard stories of affairs—the root cause was selfishness.

I've listened to spouses complain about financial infidelity—selfishness.

I have even interacted with individuals who share that they've fallen out of love—again, selfishness.

I have found that selfishness can be a major problem in the thirty-one to forty time period, and if it's not dealt with, a disaster likely awaits the individual when they reach the forty-one to fifty timeframe.

Philippians 2:3 states, "Do nothing from selfishness or empty conceit [through factional motives, or

The Stages of the Green Room

strife], but with [an attitude of] humility [being neither arrogant nor self-righteous], regard others as more important than yourselves" (AMP).

If men and women use this scripture as the bedrock of their lives, selfishness will not have the sustenance to grow, breed, and take root.

I believe selfishness is rampant during this time of life because it's not adequately prepared for during the twenty-one to thirty timeframe.

In my twenties, I was selfish.

I had spent the last 10 years of my life of raising children, going from job to job, but I had not properly prepared for the tests of manhood.

The only encouragement my father gave me was, "You'll never amount to anything!"

My father-in-law said, "You can't afford my daughter," and my mother-in-law openly told me she hated me and if I chose her daughter, I had to accept her as family!

With ten years under my belt, I felt that I had lived up to all of their expectations of me.

So, what does one do when the whole world is

watching you blow through and fail at thirty?

I prayed and began to ask God for wisdom, and thankfully my wife believed in me when no one else did.

I remember one night her rubbing my back and speaking words of life in my ear while I slept.

I realized, I tried to live up to everyone's expectations, but I could not live up to their expectations because I never asked God what He wanted from me.

One day while preaching the Lord gave me Psalm 22:5, "They cried out to You and were delivered; they trusted in You and were not disappointed or ashamed" (AMP).

This scripture changed my life.

That evening, my wife and I had a "come to Jesus meeting," and we decided that we were going to trust in God.

Everybody laughed at us for our bold stance, but we decided we were not going to live a life as victims, but as victors.

My wife and I decided we were too talented to remain poor, so we were determined to do something about

The Stages of the Green Room

it.

My wife started her own daycare.

The townspeople in Sealy, Texas would not allow her to rent a building where we lived because of our race.

Denise didn't allow their hate to stop her. She changed locations, rented a building, and started providing childcare services.

People throughout the city hated the fact that a non-credentialed, African American woman, started a business in the community.

People tried at every turn to get us to close the doors, but Denise was determined.

She worked day and night to obtain her license to ensure Denise Hall's Christian Daycare remained in business.

Eventually, we had to go to court because the neighbors signed a petition to halt our progress.

We were called before the residential commissioner.

Our entire church family showed up at the city meeting to support us.

When it was our turn to speak, I went up to the mic and asked, "Can you all tell them why we can go to church, school, and grocery stores together, but we can't conduct business together?"

During a recess, a man came to me and said if I'd let the case go, he would give me a piece of property.

We dropped the case, and he gave us the property.

The great men of Apostolic Lighthouse boarded vans and planes to help us build a beautiful church and daycare.

To this day, I am grateful for the sacrifice of Pastor Charles Hurst.

Simultaneously, while the dust was settling with Denise's business, I found an old barbeque pit and started my business.

At the time, I didn't know the first thing about barbeque, but God gave me a recipe for a special sauce, and Heaven's Best Bar-b-q sauce was born!

I am sharing these stories because it's important not to give up on yourself, even if you've made horrible decisions.

You must get over yourself, fight selfishness, and

The Stages of the Green Room

find a way to make someone's life better.

Our willingness to serve others and remain committed has worked for my wife and me. Today, we are abundantly blessed.

Initially, in my thirties, I did not know I needed to use my gifts and talents to make our lives better. I didn't know to take care of my mental, physical, and emotional self.

I missed clues that led to heartbreak and eventually, two heart attacks later in life.

I've said several times that if a person misses a season or fumbles a season, they'll pay for it in the next season.

Because a man or woman has strength and knowledge, it's easy to miss the lessons of wisdom. Focus on others, let go of selfishness, and watch life give you every dream you've dreamt.

The Years of Influence: Ages 41-50
When I turned 40, the Lord had me ready for the toughest assignment I could imagine.

A friend of mine called and asked me to play the organ for him in an all-white church organization. He was my friend, I thought it would be great, so I agreed to go.

He called me a couple of days before the event and shared a few ways he needed me to prepare for the event.

First, he asked me to shave off all of my facial hair. I was flabbergasted!

Then he told me I'd needed to take off all of my jewelry, including my wedding ring.

At first, I bucked against their requests.

My friend encouraged me that my facial hair and jewelry shouldn't get in the way of what God was doing in my life. I calmed down and did as he asked.

I can't tell you how furious I was about it at first, but it was a little thing to ask for based on the call on my life.

We went to the event, I played the organ, and the Lord moved in miraculous ways throughout the service.

Because of my attitude, my friend began to ask me to travel with him to play at big conferences. I agreed although I didn't agree with their stance on jewelry and facial hair.

The Stages of the Green Room

By forty, you should have insight into the bigger picture—understanding what God is doing in your life and that it doesn't come without a cost.

If I had still been operating in my selfish years (like I did early on in my thirties), I would have missed what God was doing in my life, and today I would likely regret forfeiting that season of unprecedented favor.

My act of obedience has taken me all over the world and broadened my perspective and influence.

It took me 40 years to have proper alignment in my life with wisdom, strength, and power. As a result, I was prepared to support others.

I realized it was not all about me, and the time to plant and be influential in someone else's life had arrived.

In your 30's, people look at you as being a young person who's trying to find his or her way, but by age 40, there is an expectation that you know something about the rhythm of life and are better positioned to support others.

The lessons I learned from forty-one to fifty helped me grow as an individual.

I learned that fear can become your greatest enemy if you allow it! I also learned that it's critical to release people who should no longer be a part of your life, so they don't become permanent fixtures in your life by fifty!

Finally, I found that forty is a time to reintroduce yourself as a person of influence with your children, rather than authority.

Be mindful that the relationship you have with your children at this stage will impact the relationship you have with your grandchildren, so tread lightly.

If a man or woman does not rid themselves of selfishness during their thirties, they enter their forties as a manipulator versus an influencer.

A manipulator is a person who has a "get them before they get me" mentality.

Manipulation is not just a worldly concept; it rears its ugly head in ministry also.

For example, I've watched a lot of men and women in ministry miss the importance of their actions.

Rather than putting their families first, ministry trumped those closest to them, causing them to lose their spouse and children.

The Stages of the Green Room

It's manipulation to believe that you are doing your work in the name of the Lord, only to lose the very people He blessed you to do life with.

I've always said that before I'd lose my family, I'd walk away from ministry.

The Concrete of Life: Ages 51-60
On my fiftieth birthday, we made a decision to shift our residence, so we were off to a new location. While we changed locations, who we were did not shift.

With a half of a century under my belt, I felt settled and seasoned.

I felt that people were waiting to hear my thoughts, understand my position, and found value in my stance towards issues and topics they faced.

The timespan of 51-60 highlights what has become solid and permanent in our lives based on the choices we've made over time.

By fifty, there is not a lot of movement or change.

Therefore, the people we are connected to matters hugely because we are no longer in the space of creating who we will become.

More specifically, during this time, we are not trying to prove anything.

Trends are no longer a barometer, as fifty-one to sixty becomes the concrete of life.

We are on autopilot, and wisdom should flow out of your life as a father/mother and mentor.

As a mentor, you are concerned with output—the results you see from life. Inputs no longer drive your actions or behaviors. Individuals who are still attempting to fill their lives at this stage are often selfish and self-centered, which is unfortunate.

If individuals have not considered their choices leading up to fifty-one to sixty, it is likely that the things that are cemented in their lives do not hold great value.

During this stage of life, my wife and I were excited to meet random people, pray for marriages, and invest deeply in relationships that mattered to us because we were solidified in who we were, and we wanted to make deposits.

The energy and drive you have at this juncture should be used to affirm and build up the generations behind you.

The Stages of the Green Room

It's a time to slow down and give the wisdom you have acquired to others, so they can begin to take on the mantle.

From fifty-one to sixty, if what you have concretized is of value, you will find that others are seeking you as a mentor and advisor because they recognize the wisdom you possess.

The Years of Honor: Ages 61 -70
On December 29, 2018, I asked myself, "Where did the time go?"

I was no longer in my 50's! The funny thing is that I had just mastered my 50's; I was settling in and ready to enjoy those years.

BAM! Just like that, I was 60 years old!

When I woke up that morning, I was somewhat emotional because I didn't know what to do in my sixties! Sixty was new to me.

I felt unprepared. No one had taught me how to navigate the sixties, nor was there a class that taught me how to move and remain effective as a 60-year-old man.

Instantly, I had to come up with a plan to ensure my

wife and I enjoyed this time of our lives. Truthfully, I hadn't enjoyed getting older at any other age, but there was a sense of peace that I experienced at sixty.

I felt confident the Lord was saying my sixties would be the years of honor.

When I started serving in ministry, I was 19 years old. My wife and I really enjoyed serving the Lord, and at times we enjoyed serving the people.

No matter how we felt, we served with class and distinction because we knew we were working for God.

We raised our children the best way we could, and we have no regrets.

We started at least eight churches across America, traveled internationally for many years, and we filled pastoral, parental, advisory, entrepreneurial, and many other roles leading up to sixty.

However, once I reached 60 years old, things changed instantly. My health mattered more, the implications of wealth increased, and the legacy I want in place has great significance.

While you must write your plan, I found those three areas were crucial for that stage of my life, and I can

The Stages of the Green Room

see how the other stages of life have led me to where I am today.

Health

When I turned 60 years old, my health was horrible. Nothing else matters if your health is bad.

I had high blood pressure, diabetes, and my blood sugar was off the charts. I was severely overweight, very tired, very depressed, yet I felt like I was living life in Jesus' name.

I am fortunate to have witnessed changes in the lives of so many people during my time in ministry; however, I hated going to the doctor, getting physicals, and learning more about the changes my body would experience.

Granted, when I finally slowed down and went to see a doctor, the doctor looked at me and said, "Mr. Hall, you are going to have to take in less salt, lose weight, get your blood pressure under control, and you must exercise!"

In the beginning, I didn't listen.

However, after a stint with chest pains and sitting in the emergency room (ER) another night, the doctor made sure I understood just how important my health had to become if I planned to continue living.

That night, as the doctor reviewed my chart, I recall him glancing over at me, then looking at my wife, then back at the chart.

After several minutes of reviewing the chart, he looked at me and asked, "Who is this beautiful woman?"

Initially caught off guard because I assumed his question was going to be about how I felt (which I shared earlier, it's not about how we feel, when we need an intervention, it's about what has occurred, so we have a chance to change the situation).

Understanding I was caught off-guard by his question, he asked again, "Who is this beautiful woman?"

Smiling, I proudly answered, "She's my wife!"

His faced changed expressions, and with all seriousness, he looked at me and said, "Mr. Hall, you spend way too much time in the ER with the same problem. Here is the truth; no one makes pills for stress.

There is no pill to make you lose weight, no medicine to make you exercise.

The Stages of the Green Room

If you don't get control over your health, you are going to drop dead, and someone else will be in your bed enjoying the beautiful wife you love."

Most people would have likely become offended and try to sue the hospital, but I understood wisdom was staring me in the eyes.

He said to me what others wouldn't. He said, if you are going to live a long, healthy life, it's all up to you, no one else!

Since, I have lost a lot of weight, gotten my blood pressure under control, my A1c (blood sugar) continues to improve, and I make decisions daily to live a healthy life.

Now, I honor my body by resting, eating healthy, exercising and drinking water, having physicals, and laughing. These factors are tools of wisdom that have great significance over time.

Resting: No matter what is going on in your life, be sure to get plenty of rest. We cannot deal with the pressures of life if we are consistently tired.

Find time to sit in the recliner and take a nap, even if it's for 30-minutes, rest.

Also, go to bed at a good time. Sometimes, it takes

me a while to fall asleep, but I position myself to rest. The older we become, the more our bodies need rest.

Eat healthily: Watching what we put into our bodies is essential.

For me, my wife exhibits a lot more discipline than I do when it comes to eating healthy, so I give her full authority to veto anything that I should not eat.

Because we are together every day, all day, we eat together, enjoy our meals together, and when we feel full, we don't eat one more morsel of food.

As a matter of fact, when our food arrives at the table, we ask for a to-go box.

We put half the food into the box and take the rest home for later if we get hungry.

Between the two of us, we have lost close to 100 pounds.

Eating healthy tells our bodies we care, and we want them to last and continue working and functioning correctly. Eat foods and portions that honor your body.

Exercise and drink water: Exercising helps our

The Stages of the Green Room

bodies stay agile. My wife and I purchased an Apple watch so we can see how many steps we've made each day.

Our goal is to take 10,000 steps. Depending on the day, sometimes we don't meet our goal, but we try to take as many steps as we can.

Go to the mall to take a walk or visit a park. Exercise! Keep your blood flowing. Drink plenty of water. My body can no longer handle lots of sugary drinks.

Water keeps things moving internally to ensure our blood is pumping and flowing appropriately. As we get older, finding ways to keep our bodies moving and drinking water are important.

Physicals: While it may sound gross, our bodies need and deserve internal cleanings. A good friend of mine told me he would never get his colon checked. He said, "No doctor is sticking his finger inside me."

While I understand his feelings, but the fact remains that physicals are key to living a healthy lifestyle. Therefore, getting our colon checked is an important factor.

During my last colonoscopy, the doctors found polyps had developed in my colon, so they removed them during the procedure.

Tony Hall, Sr.

As a result of their findings, I am required to have a colonoscopy every five years, as opposed to the standard 10-year test. One way I preserve my health is by drinking colon-cleansing products.

Due to the medications I take, my food sometimes wants to stay in my body longer than I wish, so we drink hot tea to make sure everything moves every day, if you know what I mean.

Meanwhile, women get pulled on, things stuck inside them, and all kinds of other things I will never fully understand, to remain healthy.

They need and deserve us as men to handle our physical affairs, so we have the opportunity to grow old together in a healthy manner.

Laugh: I have found that the older we get, the more severe things become. Laugh! My wife and I clown around every day.

Naturally, my wife is more of a serious person, so when the atmosphere gets too deep and heavy, I make sure we laugh at whatever is happening at that moment.

Whether it's a crazy, made-up song, or watching something on television, take time to laugh at life, at each other, and yourself. Laughter makes growing older so much more fun.

Proverbs 17:22 reads, "A happy heart is good medicine, and a joyful mind causes healing, but a broken spirit dries up the bones."

Both my wife and I have experienced a lot of trauma throughout our lives, but we don't allow those experiences to dry up our bones.

We have learned to create atmospheres of laughter, which are medicine for the wounds of our past.

When life brings hardship, find a way to create laughter, it will bring peace and allow you to grow gracefully!

Honor your body by treating yourself appropriately. Find ways to prioritize your health and stick with the plan. You will be grateful you did in the long run.

Wealth
Never in my wildest dreams would I have ever imagined that I would be retired at 60 years old, especially as a troubled child who dropped out of school.

Growing up, I made major mistakes, but as I continued to get older, I did my best to remain faithful to God.

Truthfully, remaining faithful to God was the only thing I had working for me.

I did my best to work hard, worship, and touch lives for the Kingdom of God. Because of my commitment, I believe the benefits that were reserved during my youth are being manifested now.

Looking back, I am shocked to see what God has done in my life.

As a high school dropout, I always had to work extremely hard to make sure my children and my wife had a good life.

When we were in our early 20's, we served our pastor, and we served as the church's custodial staff on Sunday afternoons. There was an evening service, so after cleaning, we'd go to a nearby restaurant to share one meal with our children because we couldn't afford to eat at the church.

Someone once asked me, "Why don't you tell the pastor about your situation?"

At that time, the church was struggling, and the members were trying to raise money to ensure we kept our spot on the radio and live TV. Further, I was not compelled to share our situation with the pastor because we were there to serve and enjoy Jesus.

The Stages of the Green Room

Likewise, during that time, churches silently required women to wear stockings or knee-high pantyhose inside the church.

We didn't argue with the unspoken rule, nor did we want to present ourselves as rebellious, we just worked hard to do what was asked by our leadership.

I didn't know it at the time, but my wife would wear mismatched knee-highs because we were too poor to buy a $1.99 pair of pantyhose each week.

Yet, she never complained or made me feel bad about it; she was always so gracious and made her dresses a little longer.

If I had time to tell you all the things my dear, sweet wife did, to help her poor, struggling, immature husband, it would take the rest of this book to explain it, but she never complained or threatened to leave me because of our situation.

For so many years, we pioneered churches, preached, ministered to people all over the world, but we didn't know how we were going to keep our lights on at home.

I would never encourage anyone to live that way, so as an example to many, we speak about our experiences, hoping that others will make better choices.

Perhaps you're wondering, "Did it work out for you?"

Yes, it worked out, but it came with stress, heart issues, and children who were impacted by our extreme poverty. I would not wish that lifestyle or pressure on anyone.

God's grace and my praying wife (who put up with that nonsense) brought us through that time.

The money I made from my 30-year barbeque business still supports us today.

To that end, I am grateful that we have become disciplined enough with our spending and saving habits that I can remain in active retirement from all forms of work, and I do not have to return to the grind.

Looking back, those times in our life were tough, but I can say everything has proved to be worth it.

As a result of my previous struggles, today, I beg children to remain in school to receive their high school diplomas.

I encourage them to continue their studies and to

The Stages of the Green Room

achieve their college degree, so they won't have to work and struggle as I did as a child or adult.

Because we have been able to retire in our sixties, we have also learned to stay within our means.

I give the money to my wife because neither of us trusts me with our money. Therefore, my wife has the veto pen regarding what we can or cannot purchase.

Sometimes I pout and throw a tantrum, but she stands her ground as the adult in the room.

Her role in our finances is critical because she makes sure that we are not living a stressful life, that our bills are paid on time, and that our savings are in tack.
She makes certain that we enjoy this stage of life and that we experience peace financially.

Denise and I have always wanted to obey the voice of God and go anywhere He calls us to go, help anyone He calls us to help, and still live a stress-free life.

It's important to ensure we are disciplined, so God can use us as He deems necessary.

We believe that the vow we made to the Lord is still in tack, and we will be able to touch more lives today than we ever have, without wondering how we will live.

Having a solid plan and foundation with our money is critical at this stage and every stage of life, as we are paying for our choices all along the way.

Much like the attention we give to our finances, we also want to be mindful that we are consistently living out our legacy.

Legacy
Legacy is defined as something handed down or received from an ancestor or predecessor. Based on the way we live our lives, we are either building a legacy that we don't want remembered, or we are building one that will allow us to be honored while we are still alive to receive the honor being given.

Therefore, at this stage of life, the question becomes, are you honored?

Honor brings praise and bestows respect and esteem on you.

I am grateful that during this stage of my life, I am admired and respected. However, the crazy thing is that I'm not always certain that I am worthy of what I am receiving.

The Stages of the Green Room

For example, when I was 27 years old, a young man named Quincy Bell entered into our lives. He was 16 years old at the time.

When he arrived from Mangham, Louisiana, he was a troubled teen, he had no relationship with his father, and as a result, his mother sent him to Job Corp.

I was tough on Quincy, but I did my best to teach him about God and life.

Looking back, it alarms me to think about how little I knew during that time of my life, but my wife and I deeply wanted to make an impact on others for God.

In 1989, when we moved to Tulsa, Oklahoma, we believed we would never see Quincy again. We were wrong!

Quincy found us in 1993, and he continued to refer to me as a father and my wife as his second mom.

My wife taught him about the power of prayer and how to commit his ways to the Lord.

She also taught him how to love and receive me as a male figure in his life, and although he did his best to listen to my words, his anger oftentimes kept him from seizing opportunities to be obedient to things I shared with him.

After my wife and I moved back home in 1997, we had completely lost contact with Quincy.

However, I often wondered what became of him, especially during my fifties (the fathering and mentoring years).

During that time in my life, I felt like I had so much to offer him from the perspective of a father, but we didn't have any contact. I wondered if the relationship we had established in prior years had enough substance to make a lasting impact.

Years later, I learned that our influence never left him. Earlier in 2019, I received a call that changed me forever.

When I answered the phone, I was stunned to hear Quincy Bell's voice on the other line.

He shared that he saw us on Facebook, found our number through mutual acquaintances, and he had to call.

"I want to thank you for leading me over the years and through some of the toughest times in my life," he said.

The Stages of the Green Room

Quincy shared the importance his mother placed on reconnecting with us, during her illness, as his spiritual mother and father.

After her death, he became determined to locate us, and he expressed so much gratitude for our lives and our love towards him.

Although we weren't there with Quincy every step of the way, our voices and influences remained with him throughout each stage of his life.

Today, he is a Godly man, serves his pastor, and gives credit to Denise and me for taking him in at such a young age.

Quincy's acknowledgment of and respect for us is a beautiful display of honor.

There are so many men and women who show honor to the things we've done in their lives.

Honor is the "thank you" from a generation that has been impacted by your words, your service, your time, or your contribution.

Honor is the fuel that keeps us going when we are forced to look at what we are no longer capable of doing.

Unfortunately, I believe there are so many men and women who are depressed because they have become jealous onlookers—vying for the spotlight that others now own.

That space of emptiness often leaves them trying to create another form of fame and glory. However, their season to establish the foundation of honor has passed.

The Bible teaches us that everything has a season. If our window of opportunity has come, when it is gone, it's very likely that we will become stuck in that season of our lives and live in disarray.

From ages 61-70, it's time for the people in our lives, those we've impacted, to praise us for the work we've done.

It's true, by this stage of life, we've done a lot of amazing things, but now we are in the bleachers, celebrating those we've touched.

I will never be a rich man with fame and fortune, but I am honored by those I've impacted; knowing my service and sacrifice to them brings my heart great joy.

Today, I like to practice honor in three main areas of my life: my marriage, in ministry, and as a father.

The Stages of the Green Room

Hebrews 13:4 reads, "marriage should be honorable by all." It saddens me to see older men and women who do not have someone madly in love with them. Similarly, my heart breaks when I realize I don't know nearly the same number of honorable marriages.

Our youngest daughter shared that she told her husband she understands the day will come when my wife and I go home to be with the Lord. However, she hopes that I will die first because I won't survive without her mom.

Guess what?

She's right!

Some may believe her words are horrible, but I view her thoughts as a statement of honor. She knows, as I believe others know as well, there is nothing or no one I adore more on this planet than my soul mate, Denise Lenora Hall.

No matter where we go, people see and applaud the love we show to each other.

Honor in marriage is a biblical mandate, and a principle I'm proud to live out each and every day.

Ministry is also a place to show honor.

Tony Hall, Sr.

After years of ministry, we retired from our role as pastors because we believed we had given all we could to the amazing people at Conquerors Church.

For us, ministry work was not a part-time job. It was and is a full-time opportunity to acknowledge and celebrate the call God has placed on our lives.

To that end, when God decided it was time for us to step aside, we did with ease because we knew we had fulfilled His assignment for our lives.

However, during our transition, we were notably celebrated for our commitment to the people God called us to shepherd.

Finally, I believe honor is important throughout our years of parenthood.

I take great joy in knowing that we have some pretty amazing kids: Darrell Alexander, Anthony Jr., Felicia Hall Bramwell, and April N. Savage. I love my children dearly, and I pray for them daily. Along with our children, we also have spiritual sons and daughters.

Most of our spiritual sons and daughters don't have fathers who are present in their lives, and some of them don't have an example of what Godly love is all about. God has placed on my life, the ability to love and lead them with the Godly love of a father. Many of them have children who honor us as grandparents.

We love them and live a life that fills the place a father should.

I believe we are honored by the children God has allowed us to bring into this world and those He's placed in our lives because of the love and care we show them.

We have done our very best to respect our children, live upright before them, and model Godly principles to show and share our deep commitment to our Heavenly Father.

Being honored from ages 61-70 is predicated on our response to the way we have treated others, the life we have lived loving our spouse, the way we have given to our call, and the people we have been in front of our children.

When we have shown honor and allowed wisdom to guide us at every stage of life, we can rest knowing our health, wealth, and legacy will be memorialized.

Tony Hall, Sr.

Endorsements

After reading his book *10 Things I Wish My Father Would Have Taught Me*, more than a couple of times and raving over it, I have naturally come to expect a high degree of excellence, transparency, and honesty from Bishop Tony Hall. The pursuit of Godly wisdom has been a wellspring of blessings for the Bishop, so again, I expect this latest offering to be nothing less than an "anointed roadmap" of wisdom to all who read it!

Ronson C. Hall
Senior Pastor, True Light Christian Fellowship
San Antonio, Texas

His stories and insights on wisdom paint pictures with a raw, honest brilliance that the world needs to hear.

May this book inspire you to dream, launch you into action, and reignite your fire in the faith—let God guide you in wisdom. Reroute your GPS, saints!

Rayven White

The saying is, "knowledge is power." While the saying is true, I believe wisdom is better! As you read this book, it will cause you to navigate to a greater destiny. Bishop Hall, thank you for sharing your life stories with us. Your words help us to grow wiser daily.

Pastor Dave Johnson

Transforming wisdom is forged in the crucible of life's experiences, both difficult and exhilarating. My brother has allowed his many life experiences, even some of his traumatic encounters from our upbringing in Detroit, to transform him into a man of wisdom. I encourage you to read this with a pen, a journal, and a highlighter. His words can't help but transform you too.

Brian K Hall

About the Author

Born and raised in the violent streets of Detroit, Michigan, Tony Hall accepted Jesus as his Savior at age fifteen. Ridiculed by his family and gang member friends he had embraced as a child, he accepted the call to preach the good news at 19-years-old.

Hall began to pastor in 1985 in the inner city of Tulsa, Oklahoma, and immediately found himself drawn to those whose lives were shattered and broken.

After a few years, his journey led him to Houston,

Texas.

Over the next several years, he founded many churches throughout Houston, and he also established work opportunities for Hispanic families in Sealy, Texas.

Traveling across the United States and around the world to places such as Africa, Canada, France, Jamaica, the Philippines, and Spain, Hall ministered to pastors and leaders, equipping them with the tools needed to grow effective churches.

Using life's experiences and his background as a pastor, he designed seminars to help couples rekindle their passion for marriage. As a result, he's been able to give real hope to couples around the world.

Bishop Hall is an ordained minister and current member of the Shield of Faith, Inc., an organization based in Pomona, California. The organization oversees nearly 1000 para-church organizations around the world.

He also oversees many churches across the United States, providing spiritual guidance to pastors and their families.

He currently serves as the CEO of Next Chapter Ministries, which is a 501c3 organization that has

About the Author

been called to help hurting pastors and to strengthen broken marriages.

In 2013, Hall was appointed by Governor Pat McCrory to serve on the Board for the Department of Social Services, as Commissioner representing eight counties in North Carolina.

Tony and wife, Denise, currently reside in Kannapolis, North Carolina. They have four adult children: Darrell, Anthony Jr. (Jennifer), Felicia (Andrew), and April (Troy). They also have fourteen awesome grandchildren and five great-grandchildren. Likewise, Tony and Denise have many spiritual sons and daughters around the world.

Connect with Tony Hall, Sr. at
www.asktonyhall.com.

www.ingramcontent.com/pod-product-compliance
Lightning Source LLC
Chambersburg PA
CBHW050439010526
44118CB00013B/1600